P9-BIC-596

THE ECONOMY OF MEXICO

ERICA M. STOKES

A cruise ship docks in a port off the Mexican coast. Tourism is an important source of income for many people in Mexico.

THE ECONOMY OF MEXICO

ERICA M. STOKES

Mason Crest Publishers
Philadelphia

Mason Crest Publishers
370 Reed Road
Broomall PA 19008
www.masoncrest.com

First printing

1 3 5 7 9 8 6 4 2

Library of Congress Cataloging-in-Publication Data on file at the Library of Congress

ISBN 1-59084-083-6

TABLE OF CONTENTS

THE ECONOMY OF MEXICO
FAMOUS PEOPLE OF MEXICO
THE FESTIVALS OF MEXICO
THE FOOD OF MEXICO
THE GEOGRAPHY OF MEXICO
THE GOVERNMENT OF MEXICO
THE HISTORY OF MEXICO
MEXICAN ART AND ARCHITECTURE
THE PEOPLE OF MEXICO
SPORTS OF MEXICO

THE GULF STATES OF MEXICO
THE STATES OF NORTHERN MEXICO
THE PACIFIC SOUTH STATES OF MEXICO
THE STATES OF CENTRAL MEXICO
THE PACIFIC NORTH STATES OF MEXICO
MEXICO: FACTS AND FIGURES

Roger E. Hernández
Senior Consulting Editor

INTRODUCTION

exico is a country in the midst of great change. And what happens in Mexico will have an important impact on the United States, its neighbor to the north.

These changes are being put in place by President Vicente Fox, who was elected in 2000. For the previous 71 years, power had been held by presidents from one single party, known in Spanish as *Partido Revolucionario Institucional* (Institutional Revolutionary Party, or PRI). Some of those presidents have been accused of corruption. President Fox, from a different party called *Partido de Acción Nacional* (National Action Party, or PAN), says he wants to eliminate that corruption. He also wants to have a friendlier relationship with the United States, and for American businesses to increase trade with Mexico. That will create more jobs, he says, and decrease poverty—which in turn will mean fewer Mexicans will find themselves forced to emigrate in search of a better life.

But it would be wrong to think of Mexico as nothing more than a poor country. Mexico has given the world some of its greatest artists and writers. Carlos Fuentes is considered one of the greatest living novelists, and poet-essayist Octavio Paz was awarded the Nobel Prize for Literature in 1990, the most prestigious honor a writer can win. Painters such as Diego Rivera and José Clemente Orozco specialized in murals, huge paintings done on walls that tell of the history of the nation. Another famous Mexican painter, Rufino Tamayo, blended the "cubist" style of modern European painters like Picasso with native folk themes.

Tamayo's paintings in many ways symbolize what Mexico is: A blend of the culture of Europe (more specifically, its Spanish version) and the indigenous cultures that predated the arrival of Columbus.

Those cultures were thriving even 3,000 years ago, when the Olmec people built imposing monuments that survive to this day in what are now the states of Tabasco and Veracruz. Later and further to the south in the Yucatán Peninsula, the Maya civilization flourished. They constructed cities in the midst of the jungle, complete with huge temples, courts in which ball games were played, and highly accurate calendars intricately carved in stone pillars. For some mysterious reason, the Mayans abandoned most of these great centers 1,100 years ago.

The Toltecs, in central Mexico, were the next major civilization. They were followed by the Aztecs. It was the Aztecs who built the city of Tenochitlán in the middle of a lake in what is now Mexico City, with long causeways connecting it to the mainland. By the early 1500s it was one of the largest cities anywhere, with perhaps 200,000 inhabitants.

Then the Spanish came. In 1519, twenty-seven years after Columbus arrived in the Americas, Hernán Cortés landed in Yucatán with just 600 soldiers plus a few cannons and horses. They marched inland, gaining allies as they went along among indigenous peoples who resented being ruled by the Aztecs. Within two years Cortés and the Spaniards ruled Mexico. They had conquered the Aztec Empire and devastated their great capital.

It was in that destruction that modern Mexico was born. The influence of the Aztecs and other indigenous people did not disappear even though untold numbers were killed. But neither can Mexico be recognized today without the Spanish influence.

Spain ruled for three centuries. Then in 1810 Mexicans began a struggle for independence from colonial Spain, much like the United States had fought for its own independence from Great Britain. In 1821 Mexico finally became an independent nation.

The newly born republic faced many difficulties. There was much poverty, especially among descendants of indigenous peoples; most of the wealth and political power was in the hands of a small elite of Spanish ancestry. To make things worse, Mexico lost almost half of its territory to the United States in a war that lasted from 1846 to 1848. Many still resent the loss of territory, which accounts for lingering anti-American sentiments among some Mexicans. The country was later occupied by France, but under national hero Benito Juárez Mexico regained its independence in 1867.

The next turning point in Mexican history came in 1911, when a revolution meant to help the millions of Mexicans stuck in poverty began against dictator Porfirio Díaz. There was violence and fighting until 1929, when Plutarco Elías Calles founded what was to become the *Partido Revolucionario Institucional*. It brought stability as well as economic progress. Yet millions of Mexicans remained in poverty, and as time went on PRI rulers became increasingly corrupt.

It was the desire of the people of Mexico to trust someone other than the candidate of PRI that resulted in the election of Fox. And so this nation of more than 100 million, with its ancient heritage, its diverse mestizo culture, its grinding poverty, and its glorious arts, stands on the brink of a new era. Modern Mexico is seeking a place as the leader of all Latin America, an ally of the United States, and an important voice in global politics. For that to happen, Mexico must narrow the gap between the rich and poor and bring more people in the middle class. It will be interesting to watch as Fox and the Mexican people work to bring their country into the first rank of nations.

Que el poder
sirva a la GENTE
VOTA
LABASTIDA
2000
.org.mx
BILLETEROS
LABASTIDA 2000
MARIO MONTES AGUILERA

1

A TROUBLED HISTORY

Mexico was not always a major player in the global world of finances. First, it was a land of native people with a primitive economy. Agriculture was the main foundation of the Aztec, Mayan, and Olmec Indian economy. Crops and livestock still bring in dollars today, but when the Spaniards arrived in the early 1500s, the economy began to change. However, Mexico did not become a nation until 1821, and it had many different governments in the next 30 years; these years of political upheaval kept its economy from growing as much as it might have.

In 1877, however, General Porfirio Díaz became president, and some historians believe he was the creator of today's Mexican economy.

Francisco Labastida was the Institutional Revolutionary Party (PRI) candidate in Mexico's most recent presidential election. His party had ruled Mexico for the past seven decades. However, Vicente Fox, of the opposing National Action Party (PAN), was elected in 2000, leading to the opportunity for political change and economic growth in Mexico.

During his term, many railroads and shipping ports were built. He united economic leaders, and as a result, farming, mining, and industries grew, and a banking system was developed.

This period, often referred to as the "Porfiriato," brought economic stability and growth. Unfortunately, however, the rich were the only ones who benefited from Díaz's economy. Many people wanted everyone to be able to earn more money. These people grew angry. The middle-class supporters of this movement eventually sent Díaz into ***exile***.

The next years saw many fights. The disputes turned ugly, and ***civil* war** broke out. The *Partido Revolucionario Institucional* (PRI), which translates to the Institutional Revolutionary Party, formed in 1929. This political party fought for the rights of workers and common people. During these years, Mexicans developed a fierce sense of ***nationalism***.

In 1934, Lazaro Cardenas became president. During his administration, the government became more active in the economy. More crops were grown; private investments slowed; and the government took over the railroads. Now working class people could make more money.

Throughout the 1940s, the PRI controlled the economy. The PRI made the nation's decisions, and under its leadership the economy grew. But the rich began taking control back from the working class, and once again the common people began to be unhappy.

The term that a Mexican president serves is called a *sexenio*. This means that the president will be in office for six years.

Stability returned in the 1950s. The costs of goods and services leveled off. Mexican commodities—products sold or

Porfirio Díaz presided over Mexico from 1877 to 1911. He influenced many aspects of Mexican life, but his regime was devoted primarily to the economic development of the country.

Former Mexican president Luis Echeverria speaks during a press conference in 1979. Echeverria was one of the representatives of the more than 100 countries that participated in the UN World Food Conference.

traded—evened out too, thanks to Mexico's Central Bank and Treasury. This federal agency ordered that ***tariffs*** on imported goods be higher. It also set limits on ***imports***, and it managed prices.

Problems arose in the late 1960s, though. Mexico was exporting goods, but that was not enough. The nation's imports were costing more than the ***exports*** it brought in. Since Mexico imported more goods than it exported, this meant that the economy suffered. Debts mounted up.

People can run short of the money they need to pay their bills, and so can countries. Like people, nations have to pay back the money they have borrowed. But a country may not have enough cash to pay back all it owes. The amount of extra cash it would need to pay it all is called a deficit. In Mexico in 1961, the national deficit was $261 million. By 1970, Mexico was short $1 billion. Meanwhile, the poor and middle class felt left out of politics. This tension sharpened the nation's economic struggles.

In 1970, Luis Echeverria became president. He wanted to shape up the economy. He improved public schools and medical clinics; he used public funds to pay for projects; and he gave the government more control. But his tactics did not work for long. He took too much from his country's revenues, and ***inflation*** rose. The Mexican ***peso*** lost 40 percent of its value in 1976. Now the country faced a financial emergency. Reluctantly, Echeverria signed an agreement with an organization called the International Monetary Fund (IMF). This contract helped Mexico. The plan gave it enough money to rebuild their economy.

But the once thriving country was still in trouble. In fact, Mexico now faced economic ruin. The new president, Jose Lopez Portillo, did not help. He did not try to regulate the peso's value, and he did not rebuild his country's nest egg. Instead, he borrowed even more money.

Mexico was rich in oil, however, and when oil prices jumped in 1979, it seemed like the money would roll in. Many countries loaned the struggling nation money, because they thought Mexico would export so much oil that it would be able to easily pay back its loans. But instead of putting the loaned money to good use, the government ignored the economy's problems. Things got still worse. These actions would haunt Mexico into the next decade.

Global ***interest rates*** rose in the early 1980s. This setback caused a U.S. ***recession***, which meant that the United States could no longer afford so many Mexican exports. Since Mexico depended on the

Jimmy Carter poses with Jose Lopez Portillo at the White House in the late 1970s. The two leaders were meeting to discuss the issue of energy. Some of Portillo's bad decisions weakened Mexico's economy.

United States market for its exports, the Mexican economy went from bad to worse. Another blow came in 1982, when the price of oil dropped. A final kick came near the end of Portillo's term when he nationalized the bank, giving the government control of the banks. The economy was in real trouble now.

2

FINDING SOLUTIONS

The next president, Miguel de la Madrid Hurtado, tried to paddle his country out of the deep sea of debt. His new tax strategy cut down on revenue loss. The tax structure was easier to follow, and he reduced government spending. His administration devalued the peso and raised interest rates. The government increased taxes, and made gas and electricity more expensive. These changes helped rebuild the economy. The new president also helped mend relationships between businessmen and officials.

Under President Madrid, Mexico entered the General Agreement on Tariffs and Trade (GATT) in 1986. GATT opened the economy. It reduced import tariffs, and trading with foreign countries grew. Mexican industries now had to compete with imported goods, so Mexican merchants sold better products at lowered prices. And in 1987, the

Having made the chaotic economy a priority during his campaign for Mexico's presidency, Carlos Salinas was able to do very little to improve it. His early tactics of economic reform, such as privatization of industry, were successful. Unfortunately, the declining value of the peso created an economic collapse in Mexico, and Salinas fled the country.

Economic Solidarity Pact (PSE) began. The PSE helped the economy grow, and inflation dropped.

When Carlos Salinas de Gortari was elected president in 1988, he continued to build on de la Madrid's improvements. He vowed to reach economic goals that would ease the economic suffering of his people. To do this, he collected more taxes from the people, so that he did not have to borrow more money from other countries. He followed the Pact for Growth and Economic Stability, and he sold corporations that the government owned to pay for more repairs. Under his leadership, fewer officials became crooked, and Mexico came up with a plan to reduce its debt. Partly in response to this plan, U.S. treasury secretary Nicolas Brady offered a new solution in 1989.

This solution was called the Brady Plan. The plan put the struggling economy on the plus side, and it paved the way for re-growth. The strategy made it less risky for lenders to give Mexico credit, so the government could borrow at lower interest rates. This way, Mexicans had money to back them up.

Meanwhile, Salinas freed the banks from government control. In a State of the Nation address, he said, "A state with too much property, with so many resources tied up in banks, is unacceptable when it has so many other demands to attend to. Now the resources from the bank sale and additional resources which will not have to be used to modernize banking can be used to respond to more pressing demands of the Mexican people."

To unlock more funds, Salinas had an idea. He thought of a new way to build highways. In the past, the government had built all the roads

Nicolas Brady, the U.S. secretary of the treasury, displays a giant dollar bill with his signature on it. In 1989, Brady offered a plan to President Salinas to get his country's economy back on its feet.

in Mexico. Now, Salinas let investors build toll roads. These are roads that charge drivers a fee, and this way, companies earned a profit.

Salinas made sure that public money was used to build better industries. The tax structure kept changing for the better, and the cost of goods and services evened off. By 1993, inflation had been lowered to 10 percent, and the foreign debt reduced by some $25 billion. His strides helped other troubled countries, because nations in debt could learn from Mexico.

When he became president of Mexico in 1994, Ernesto Zedillo inherited a disordered economy and an enormous national debt. Although he did what he could to improve the situation, much work lies ahead for future leaders.

But Salinas did not stop improving Mexico. He wanted to lure foreign companies and modern technology to Mexico so that his people could get better jobs. Some people did not like his plan, though. They feared that businesses like Wal-Marts and Burger Kings would destroy family businesses. But Salinas responded that a free-trade agreement was "the only way I can respond to the interests of the 82 million Mexicans today and the almost two million that are added each year."

The North American Free Trade Agreement (NAFTA) came about in 1992. U.S. President Bush, Canadian Prime Minister Mulroney, and Mexican President Salinas all signed NAFTA. It was approved in 1993, and it took effect in 1994. The agreement allows goods and services to be traded freely without barriers between member countries. Each member country may set its own policy regarding trade with nonmember countries.

Over the next 10 to 15 years, the goals of NAFTA are:

- Get rid of anything that holds up trade between Canada, the United States, and Mexico.
- Spur fair competition between the member nations.
- Allow more areas for investing.
- Set rules for settling arguments that may develop.
- Encourage the three country's governments to work together.

In 1994, when Ernesto Zedillo Ponce de León was elected president, he faced the chore of rebuilding the economy. The

Zedillo was not the first choice for president. The man who was to take Salinas' place was Luis Donaldo Colosio, but in 1994, Colosio was assassinated.

government owed many people money. Foreign companies were scared to invest in Mexico. Unfortunately, Zedillo helped cause the peso to lose more than 50 percent of its value. High interest rates kept the economy from growing. These rates put Mexico back in crisis.

In early 1995, the IMF and the United States loaned Mexico $52 billion to help. Later that year, Zedillo tightened the purse strings. He put limits on how much prices could rise. He set limits on wages too. He also cut government spending.

The cost of goods and services grew fast. But workers' wages did not grow, so people fell behind on their bills. Necessary goods and services now cost too much. And banks lacked the money needed to stay open. To help keep banks working, the government did four basic things: It took control of banks that had little or no money left. It pushed the sale of some banks by supplying funds. Then it bought any assets that did not make money from banks. And it offered programs to help people who might go into debt.

Still, lack of investment and many debts pushed Mexico into a business slump. In 1996, new policies changed the way to pay back owed money. This strategy helped Mexico repay the United States, and Mexican investments increased. The federal budget stayed balanced, while Mexico's deals with other countries boomed. The economy grew faster than at any other time in recorded Mexican history.

Mexico can trade with many countries. It joined the Asia-Pacific Economic Cooperation (APEC) in 1993. It joined the Organization for Economic Cooperation and Development (OECD) in 1994, and in 1996 it joined the World Trade Organization (WTO).

Vicente Fox shakes hands with Mexican Finance Minister Jose Angel Gurria shortly after Fox's election in 2000. The two met to discuss the financial transition resulting from the changing government, a circumstance which often causes economic turmoil.

To avoid another financial problem, finance minister Jose Angel Gurria created a plan. This strategy had six main points.

* Keep the budget deficit low and controllable.
* Stop being overtaken by debt.
* Export many types of goods to avoid becoming too dependent on one product, like oil.
* Concentrate on building up domestic savings.
* Allow the peso's value to float. Let it go up and down with the market flow.
* Keep banks healthy. Supervise and regulate as needed.

The year 1999 was a time of economic growth, thanks to the Zedillo administration. Demand for goods and services grew. Exports increased at record rates. The ***unemployment rate*** was the lowest since 1985, while inflation was the lowest since 1994. Production and investments grew, further boosting the economy.

If 1999 was good, however, the year 2000 was even better, one of the best years for Mexico. The same year, Vicente Fox Quesada became the president of Mexico.

Some of Fox's economic goals are to:

* Increase the gross domestic product.
* Encourage foreign investment, especially in the electricity industry.
* Reorganize Mexican industries.
* Become less dependent on oil as a source of export money.

* Come closer to balancing the budget.
* Reduce inflation.
* Make Mexico's savings stronger and bigger.

However, these goals may not come easily. In last months of 2000 and throughout 2001, the U.S. economy began slowing down. Since Mexico's economic success depends on the success of the U.S. economy, tougher times may lie ahead for Mexico. High oil prices helped raise the peso's value in 2000, but the when price of oil dropped in the fall of 2001, so did the peso's value. Fewer exports to the United States and low oil prices can cause inflation to rise.

Another problem will be the labor market. Industries have enough employees, so skilled workers may have trouble finding jobs. If businesses cannot sell goods and services for enough profit, wages may also decrease. These issues can cause inflation to rise.

The North American Free Trade Agreement (NAFTA) was signed into existence in 1992 by leaders of Canada, Mexico, and the United States. Mexico's president Carlos Salinas stands to the left, in front of the country's chief trade representative Julie Puche; U.S. President George Bush Sr. stands in the middle with chief trade representative Carla Hills; and Canadian Prime Minister Brian Mulroney (standing) and trade representative Michael Wilson are pictured on the right. NAFTA did not go into effect until 1994.

MANUFACTURING AND INDUSTRIES

The gross domestic product (GDP) is important to a country. The GDP is the total amount of money earned from all goods and services in a year. In 2001, Mexico's GDP amounted to nearly $400 billion, the 11th largest in the world.

To create a good economy, the GDP must grow—and to make the GDP grow, private consumption must increase. Investment must grow as well, which means Mexicans must consume products. They must invest money to keep the economy booming.

Foreign capital—in other words, foreign businesses who bring money into the country—is a way to keep the economy growing. About 10 billion dollars of investments a year are needed for 3 to 4 percent growth. As the economy grows, so must its funds.

Volkswagen, General Motors, Ford, Nissan and Chrysler have set up shop in Mexico. Car parts and big machines are shipped into Mexico. Then workers construct cars for export.

Here are three ways to feed a hungry economy:

- Keep money in savings. Mexico can use the money that people save in banks.
- Get portfolio investments. This type of investing usually comes from buying stock. Treasury certificates and investment shares can build a financial portfolio too.
- Gain foreign direct investment (FDI). Most countries like this option the best. FDI commits time and money to a nation. Once FDI comes, the economy can count on that money for a long time.

Many countries compete for FDI, so Mexico has to work hard to look like the best place for this investment. The Mexican government allows each state to offer even more ways to attract FDI. Loans and reduced taxes help attract FDI.

The Mexican Secretariat of Commerce and Industrial Development (SECOFI) approves corporations. They bring in manufacturing plants that are called *maquiladoras*. These firms can import goods without tax, if they export the finished product. For example, fabric and machines can be imported with no tax, but maquiladoras must use the fabric and machines to make something, like t-shirts. Then they have to export the t-shirts. They must also promise to send

Geography puts Mexico into the thick of things. To the north lies a 2,000-mile border with the United States, and to the south, a 700-mile border with Guatemala and Belize. Ports on the Gulf of Mexico, Caribbean Sea, and Pacific Ocean allow prime shipping to anywhere in the world.

A bank building in Mazatlan, Mexico. Due to complications and long-standing debts, Mexico's economy has been unstable for decades.

back the machines. Or they can sell the t-shirts in Mexico if they pay the import tax they would be saving.

This program began in 1965, and it continues to grow with the help of NAFTA. Maquiladoras help U.S. investors make large profits, since they do not have to pay U.S. wages, nor do they have to follow the U.S. safety regulations that cost a business time and money. For instance, if a soda factory had to pay Americans to make soda the cost of labor would be high. But if soda were made in a Mexican

Benito Juarez's likeness is featured on this Mexican bank note. The value of Mexican currency on the foreign market has been low for many years.

maquiladora, low labor costs would make more profits for the American corporation. The owners do not have to pay Mexican workers much money; they can allow unsafe conditions to exist in their factories; and it is easy to ship the products back to the nearby United States. Maquiladoras make electronics, clothing, and cars. By 1999, more than 3,500 of these plants employed about 1.2 million workers. The system does help bring foreign money into Mexico, but there is a growing concern that the laborers in maquiladoras are receiving unfair wages while they work in an environment that is unsafe.

Not all of Mexico's exports come from maquiladoras. Mexico's exports also include food and beverages; tobacco products like snuff and cigarettes; jewelry, leather goods, pottery, and clothes and woven crafts; electronic equipment and automobiles; and chemicals, iron, steel, and cement. Household goods account for some of Mexico's manufactured exports. These include foods like baby food, candy, cereals, canned food, frozen food, pre-packaged food, and pet food. Exported drinks include beer, juice, wine, liquor, milk, and soft drinks. Baby products like diapers and bottles are made in Mexico and shipped out to other countries. Everyday items like batteries, clothing, cleaning supplies, medicines, and film are exported too. By far, Mexico's most important export market is the United States, but Mexico also sells much to Canada, Spain, Japan, Venezuela, Chile, and Brazil.

But all of the money earned in 2001 from exports was not enough. Imports still cost too much. Mexico bought $142.1 billion in imports that year, nearly $5 billion more than the nation earned from its exports. More imports than exports make the economy go down and creates an unfavorable trade balance. Trade problems cost citizens money. They add to the national debt, and then the economy slows even more.

Julio Antonio Martinez Oropeza worked at a shrimp-packing plant in Nayarit. In September of 2000, he was cleaning out a tank when he breathed in toxic fumes and fainted. Four coworkers who noticed him slumped inside the tank jumped in to save him. But the fumes were too strong. All five workers died because of illegal factory operations. Owners of the plant had saved money by not following safety codes. The plant was not inspected, regulated, or licensed. Making sure the factory was safe could have saved five lives.

IN JANUARY OF 2001, ABOUT 900 SWEATSHIRT MAKERS PROTESTED AT A NIKE FACTORY IN PUEBLA. THEIR COMPLAINTS INCLUDED:

- **Raw, rotten or worm-infested cafeteria food. The food has caused diarrhea. Some workers have even been to the hospital.**
- **Not enough money. Workers may earn only 75 cents an hour.**
- **No Christmas bonus. The labor law in Mexico makes companies give workers something extra for Christmas, but the Nike factories were not obeying this law.**
- **Abuse such as name-calling or even hitting from the bosses.**
- **Failing to pay benefits for pregnant women.**
- **No extra wages for overtime.**
- **Not enough safety gear. Eyes, throats, lungs, and noses were exposed to stinging chemicals with no protective masks.**

Five workers who asked that crimes like these be stopped were fired for speaking out.

Days after the protest, police arrived at the factory. They bullied the rebels, mostly women and teenagers. About 15 workers went to the hospital because of the attack.

Mexico gets most of its imports from the United States. Other valuable trading partners are Germany, Japan, Canada, South Korea, Italy, and France. Mexico imports the steel mill equipment, agricultural machinery, automotive and airplane parts and machinery, and electrical supplies it needs for its industries. Imports like seeds, soybeans, corn, and sorghum feed people and animals. Imported ships and airplanes help transport goods. Manufactured goods, asbestos fiber, tin, and kaolin are also imported, as are industrial diamonds, calcium phosphate, and iron pipes.

Most of the nation's industrial centers and plants are in the Federal District of Mexico, the area near Mexico City. Investors like setting up factories there for many

Due to the low cost of labor in Mexico, many U.S. companies build factories south of the border. This man is constructing a vehicle on an assembly line at a Ford Motors plant in Cuautitlan.

reasons. Such a huge city is alive with potential employees, and many people are skilled. The big city also has more potential customers. Companies can sell goods almost in their backyard, and investors save money by not having to pay for mailing. This place is also home to government officials, who may make factory owners feel more at ease. Monterrey and Guadalajara are industrial spots too. Juarez, Tijuana, Veracruz, Durango, León, Queretaro, Tampico, Mérida, and Puebla also house manufacturers.

AGRICULTURE FEEDS A HUNGRY ECONOMY

In 1998, Mexico exported more than $3 billion of agricultural goods to the United States. Those exports made up 8 percent of Mexico's GDP. Farms gave jobs to nearly a quarter of all Mexican workers, which adds up to around 8 million people. America ships about 12 percent of its agricultural products to Mexico, but Mexico sends more than 60 percent of its agricultural goods back to the United States. Keep in mind that the United States has more farming land than Mexico, but Mexico still exports a greater percentage of farm products.

NAFTA helps make agriculture trade strong between the United States and Mexico. As a result, Mexican agricultural exports to the United States have grown by about 11.5 percent a year since NAFTA took effect. Vegetables and fruits continue to take the lead in Mexican agricultural exports.

The agave plant thrives in Mexico's dry, hot deserts. The pulp of the plant is used to make tequila, which is both sold in Mexico and exported to other countries.

During President Salinas' administration the government gave farmers money in times of trouble. This became the Agricultural Production Benefits Program (PROCAMPO), a program that looks out for grain (corn, wheat, sorghum) farmers and pays them if they fall on hard times. PROCAMPO also markets Mexico's agricultural crops. Extra ***promotions*** increase sales. In addition, PROCAMPO helps farmers ***conserve*** land, and teaches them how to rotate crops. These changes make harvests better.

President Zedillo ensured that PROCAMPO would be active until 2008. He also created the Alliance for Agricultural Development. The goal of this plan is to grow higher priced goods. For instance, corn is not costly—which means a farmer can earn more money by growing high-priced mangoes than he could by growing corn. And more money for the farmer means more money for Mexico. The alliance also aims to create more jobs in agriculture.

Many foreigners invest in food-processing plants, but few sink dollars into agriculture. Mexican laws are the reason for this. Most people who don't live in Mexico cannot own farms. If a farmer is too poor to buy land, the government lends them land where they can then make a living. These farms are called *ejidos*. Outsiders cannot rent them, and no corporate farming is allowed. Foreigners also cannot buy property in the Restricted Zone, the land within 62 miles of Mexico's international borders

The agave or century plant grows in the desert. Mexicans call it maguey, and they process the plant's sap to make a popular export, tequila, a strong alcoholic drink. As many as 136 types of agave grow in Mexico, but only the sap of blue agave, maguey azul, can make tequila.

Tourism is a vital part of Mexico's economy. Hotels, restaurants, craftsmen, and folk artists all make money from tourists. Even silly souvenirs bring in a few dollars.

with the United States, Belize, and Guatemala. The zone also includes land within 31 miles of Mexico's coasts.

Fresh fruits and vegetables are mainly grown in northeast Mexico. This section near Texas is very dry due to little rain. Farmers must irrigate this land with ditches and pipes. The most popular crops tend

A burro grazes on a hillside farm. Agriculture is important to the Mexican way of life. It provides both an income and a means of sustenance for many people.

to be oranges, tomatoes, apples, grapes, tangerines, grapefruit, pears, and raisins. Mexico produces plenty more food exports too—for instance, tropical fruits like bananas, mangoes, pineapples, and avocados; other fruits like lemons, limes, melons, peaches, nectarines, plums, and strawberries; and vegetables like tomatoes, green peas, green chilies, and green beans. Crops that make drinks like coffee, cocoa, and maguey are valuable to the Mexican economy also. Sweeteners like sugar and honey sell too. Cotton is important for textiles. Soybeans, peanuts, and sunflower seeds bring in money as well.

A community of peers is a vital source of support for Mexican farmers. The members of an ejido, or farming collective, sit in a large circle at a meeting.

The amount and type of crops that bring in the most money change each year. Weather, worldwide prices, and buyers' demand make a difference in Mexico's exports. In 2001, tomatoes were the top Mexican crop shipped to the United States.

One-third of Mexico became official grazing lands in the early 1990s. These ranches are now home to Herefords and other beef cattle. Livestock raised in the north are shipped to the United States, while central and southern ranchers raise cattle for Mexico. Swine (pigs), lamb, sheep, goat, and chickens are also exported, and eggs from chickens are shipped out of the country. Mexico also exports dairy products such as milk and cheese.

MEXICO BANKS ON ITS NATURAL RESOURCES

Metal production is one of Mexico's biggest ***assets***. Mining minerals helps the economy. In fact, Mexico is in the top 11 countries for 19 minerals. In 1998, Mexico produced the most silver (17 percent) in the world. It also produced the most ***celestite*** (38 percent). And it produced the most ***bismuth*** (29 percent). Mexican mines brought in the second-most ***fluorspar***, and the third most ***graphite***. Mexico also produces many other minerals: mercury, iron, arsenic, antimony, zinc, cadmium, lead, dolomite, kaolin, silica sand, phosphorite, molybdenum, barite, salt, gypsum manganese, copper, feldspar, tungsten, and sulphur are all important exports.

Fishing boats are docked for the evening in Mexico. Learning to fish is another way poor Mexicans can make a living.

Government officials approved the Mining Law Regulation in 1999. Based on this law, a new system came about. Agencies in charge of mining updated the way things ran, and policies and practices changed for the better. Rules were cut—the 1999 law got rid of 20 percent of mining procedures—but miners now knew how and when to use regulations, since the remaining regulations were easier to follow.

The mining industry exported $2.2 billion worth of metals and minerals in 1998, 1.7 percent of Mexico's total exports, while imported metals and minerals cost Mexico $1.3 billion that same year. Since the economy fairs better when a country exports more than it imports, 1998 saw a good trade balance in the mining ***sector***.

Many energy reserves are also helping the Mexican economy get back on its feet. Mexico produced 182.5 billion ***kilowatt-hours*** of power in 1999. Most of the nation's electricity comes from oil, gas, or coal. Mexico also depends on hydropower (from water); nuclear, wind, and solar resources; and biomass (from plant material).

In 1999, Mexico also imported about a billion kilowatt-hours. Altogether, Mexicans used about 164.8 billion kilowatt-hours that year. That may seem like endless power, but many Mexican homes still have no electricity. These conditions cause economists to think trouble lies ahead. As more people can afford electricity, demand may be too great. What if Mexico cannot provide electricity? Then blackouts may occur. If private investors cannot help fund growing power needs, Mexico could be in the dark.

Petroleum is another big piece of Mexico's economic puzzle. The late 19th century

Pangas are small boats that most deep-sea fishermen in Mexico use.

A uranium mines sprawls over the landscape. In order to compete globally, Mexico is learning to take advantage of its natural resources.

brought Mexico's first oil discovery. Oil has since played a major role in Mexican finances, especially after the early 1970s when oil reserves were found. The Gulf of Mexico has about 56 percent of Mexico's reserves, 24 percent are in the Chicontepec region, and 15 percent are in Tabasco and Chiapas.

The morning sun silhouettes an oil platform in the Gulf of Mexico. Industrial work has become a major source of income for skilled laborers.

By 1980, Mexico had racked up $12.6 billion of petroleum credit from the United States. This money made it possible for Mexicans to build: they could now drill offshore. They built processing plants; they looked for more oil; they bought necessary equipment, and in 1982, petroleum accounted for nearly 80 percent of all Mexico's exports. Between 1983 and 1991, these improvements helped Mexico export 1.4 million barrels of oil...per day!

Oil prices rose in the late 1980s and early 1990s, but then in 1993, Mexico's oil exports took a dive. Less production and demand brought prices down. By 1995, oil made up just 10 percent of Mexico's exports. Mexico still ranked as the world's fifth-largest oil producer, but it had fallen to 10th place by 2000. Still, in 2000, oil exports brought in $10.4 billion. Pemex (Petroleos Mexicanos) is the state oil company, the nation's most important company.

Natural gas is another resource in Mexico. The Mexican Energy Regulatory Commission (CRE) controls natural gas. This commission inspects facilities and regulates prices. It also advertises natural gas. In 1999, 1.29 trillion cubic feet (Tcf) of natural gas were produced, and 1.26 Tcf were used that year.

Most natural gas is needed in the north, but this resource is produced in the south in the waters near the Yucatán Peninsula. Pipelines help to link these places together. However, more pipelines are needed to distribute natural gas all across Mexico. CRE members are deciding how and where to lay the pipelines.

Another vital natural resource is found not in Mexico's land but its water. Since Mexico borders the Gulf of California, the Pacific Ocean, the Gulf of Tehuantepec, the Carribean Sea, the Gulf of Campeche, and the Gulf of Mexico, it's no wonder that fishing is a million-dollar industry for Mexico. Lakes, rivers, and ponds provide additional fishing grounds. In 1998, Mexicans caught 1,113,349 tons of fish, and they exported 182 tons, $716 million worth.

Next time you chew bubble gum, thank a tree. Forests produce chicle, the milky liquid that comes from some trees. Chicle is then sold as the main ingredient for chewing gum.

Shrimp made up 66 percent of these seafood export dollars. Other exports included jewfish, croaker, mackerel, snook, mullet, clams, anchovies, abalone, red snapper, lobster, octopus, and sardines.

Small boats are the main tool used to catch ocean fish. Shrimp trawlers drag nets to catch shrimp. Tuna and sardine fisherman commonly use seiners, boats that pull nets carrying weights on the bottom and floats on the top. These boats catch most of the fish caught in the Pacific Ocean.

Mexico also caught 98,000 tons of freshwater fish in 1998. The most common freshwater fish is tilapia, but carp is also popular. Other freshwater fish include prawns, bass, and trout.

Aquaculture raises aquatic creatures in a controlled environment; the Mexican industry brought in nearly 41,000 tons of fish in 1998. Shrimp was the top product in fisheries, but oysters, trout, tilapia, carp, catfish, and prawns were also grown there.

Most of the fish are sold fresh, but some are frozen or canned. The states of Sonora, Sinaloa, and Veracruz bring in the most fish.

Natural resources such as trees, soil, water, and wildlife are also essential for Mexico's economy. These resources account for over half of the region's economic production and jobs. For instance, Mexican loggers plant, grow, and chop down trees so that wood, sap, and turpentine can be exported. Mexico has more types of pine and oak trees than any other country. Pine trees are the most common, but the live oak and the fir tree bring in the most export dollars. Mexican forests are also home to cedar, primavera, sapote, copa, mahogany, ebony, rosewood, and walnut trees.

In 1997, Mexican forest areas took up 136,861 acres, and forestry exports totaled $444 million that same year. The number of tree-

The thin towers of a natural gas refinery tower above the rest of the terrain. Gas fields are often located far from major cities and towns. Natural gas is of little use in its original form, and must be processed to create its more valuable liquid and gaseous counterparts.

products imported that year was more than $1.4 billion, however, creating a negative trade balance. In other words, Mexico is exporting goods made from its forests, but it still needs to import much more for its citizens.

To improve its economy, Mexico needs to increase production of wood-based products—but the forests of Mexico face many dangers. Droughts and fires cause tree loss. Certain kinds of bugs destroy growing trees. Deforestation—when trees are cut down so that cattle can graze or crops can be planted—is also a threat to Mexican forests. Human greediness is a bigger danger to trees than any natural enemy; when trees are cut down and not properly replanted, both the economy and the environment are harmed.

MEXICO'S BEAUTY PAYS OFF

Mexico's value as a vacation spot first began to grow in the early 1900s. The Department of the Interior created a council, an official team that would aid tourism, called the Tourism Promotion Council. In the 1940s, President Aleman further helped tourism by building more roads, airports, and hotels. In 1963, the first national plan for tourism was realized when the government created the *Secretaria de Tourismo* (the Department of Tourism) and the National Tourism Promotion Fund (FONATUR). These two groups merged in 1974.

FONATUR created areas whose sole purpose was to attract vacationers. Zihuatanejo, Puerto Escondido, Ixtapa, Cancún, and Huatulco are areas that were built up as tourists' resorts, places where visitors can stay and spend money. When the peso's value went down in the late 1980s,

The crashing waves of Mexican beaches rise to meet hotels as well as ancient ruins. In recent years, Mexico has become one of the most popular vacation spots for American tourists, thanks to its location, affordability, and beautiful scenery.

ECOTOURISM MAKES "CENTS"

Regular tourism is just about having a good time. But ecotourism protects the environment. It unites people who want to learn more about and preserve the earth. It also brings profit.

Those who stay in regular hotels may not realize the damage done. An example is found in Chihuahua's Copper Canyon. The area does not have a way to dispose of waste properly, so hotel garbage may be thrown into the beautiful canyon itself. But ecotourists either camp outdoors and remove their own garbage, or they stay in the pricier hotels that take the time and money to get rid of the trash properly.

Ecotourism does two main things for the economy: First, it lures better quality tourists and their money, people who respect the environment more. And second, it protects the environment. If land is not cared for, ultimately, tourists will not come because the area has become dirty and ugly—and the economy will also suffer as a result.

money still came in from tourism. From 1987 to 1990, the number of tourists increased by 3 million.

Mexico is now one of the world's favorite places to visit, and Americans visit Mexico more than any other country in the world. Tourism helps drive the Mexican economy. Workers in tourism can earn good money, and tourism is the third largest income maker. In 2000, tourism brought in about $8 billion, and by 2010, the Mexican tourism industry GDP should have grown to $83.1 billion.

A main way tourism boosts the economy is by providing jobs. Tourism made nearly a million jobs for Mexicans in 1999. Restaurants offer jobs: people can wait tables, tend bar, bus dishes, clean, manage, and cook. Hotels also offer jobs: people can clean, work at the desk, do room service, carry bags, park cars, cook, and guard guests. Large resorts may offer jobs too: employees there can sing, play in a band, dance, teach swimming, be a

Ecotourism entrepreneur Mauricio Brittingham poses in front of a tent in the private nature reserve created by him and his partner Alberto Garza. The concept of ecotourism has been catching on in recent years, and has become a profitable venture in Mexico.

lifeguard, coach tennis, watch children, and plan activities. Other jobs are also created by tourism. For instance, workers can take tourists scuba diving, whale watching, sailing, bus touring, horseback riding, and helicopter riding.

Jobs come indirectly from tourism as well. If people don't work in a restaurant or hotel, they can still make more money due to tourists, since those who work for airlines and taxis get more business. Travel

The peak of Popocatepl volcano is daunting at nearly 18,000 feet. Many tourists and native Mexicans make the grueling hike to the top each year.

agents make more money too, as do Mexicans who make and sell crafts. Builders are also needed as restaurants and hotel chains grow. Roads, airports, water systems, and sanitation services must be improved, providing still more jobs. And more mouths need more food, so the agriculture and fishing industries also grow. Tourism can help Mexicans in many different ways.

Mexico has more than 390,000 rooms in 9,500 hotels, 15,000 tourist restaurants, 69 marinas, and 77 golf courses. In 1998, 19.3 million tourists visited places like these. This makes Mexico one of the best tourist spots in the world.

Some areas attract more tourists than others. But all can build a larger tourism business. Mexico has thousands of miles of scenic coasts that lure beachgoers. Puerto Vallarta, Cancún, Cabo San Lucas, and Acapulco are just a few of the many tropical seaside cities. The Mexican mountains and canyons are breathtaking too, and these natural wonders appeal to thrill-seekers. Mexico City offers culture, and history buffs enjoy Mexico's many archeological sites, like the Olmec ruins in Tabasco and the Mayan relics in Quintana Roo.

MEXICO OFFERS UNIQUE TOURIST ATTRACTIONS:

Kayaking next to whale sharks in Baja California.

Mountain climbing to the top of Piacacho del Diablo (Devil's Peak).

Watching Monarch butterflies as they migrate for the winter.

Hiking up the twin volcanoes, Popocatepl and Ixtaccihuatl.

Rafting down the Antigua River.

Diving the largest coral-ringed lagoon in the world.

Watching jaguars and macaws in the Sierra Gorda Biosphere Reserve.

The monarch butterfly migrates annually to mate and reproduce. Some butterflies may travel as far as 80 miles in a day. Tourists come to Mexico to see the butterflies gathering on trees to hibernate.

Nature lovers can see rare birds and mammals in rainforests, while seafarers can enjoy exotic marine life.

In the mid-1990s, tourism was seen as a great way to boost the economy. Officials came up with a policy to promote tourism still more. This system helps Mexico reap even more benefits. The overall goal was to open up the country. Leaders wanted the world to meet *el corazon*, the heart of Mexico. They wanted everyone to know the real Mexico, a land with rich culture and traditions.

The first phase of the policy aimed to develop the various regions in Mexico. By polishing up these places, the government hoped to attract more tourists. When this happens, jobs will open up. Investments will go up. And the economy will be healthy.

The second part of the policy deals with maintenance. Leaders want to make sure improvements continue. Mexican policymakers want developments nice and new looking. They also seek to bring in new projects. When this works, materials are recycled. Resources like water and energy are saved. Cultural icons are repaired. And more tourists come.

The final part of the policy is investment. Foreign investors can expand tourism. Getting people to invest helps the economy. This prevents damage to the environment. And ultimately, as the economy grows, Mexico's beauty can be preserved.

One vital Mexican tourist attraction is the handiwork of Mexican artisans. These crafts include pottery, textiles, leather goods, wooden carvings, and jewelry.

CHRONOLOGY

1519 Hernán Cortés arrives from Spain.

1810 Mexico begins fight for independence from Spain.

1821 Mexico gains independence from Spain.

1869 Mexico's first oil well is drilled.

1877 Porfirio Díaz becomes president, beginning the "Porfiriato" period.

1938 The oil industry of Mexico is nationalized.

1946 Miguel Aleman becomes president and begins fueling the economy with more highways, railroads and airports.

1963 The Department of Tourism and the National Tourism Promotion Fund are created.

1970 The Federal Labor Act takes effect; this law deals with wages and employment issues.

1982 President Portillo nationalizes Mexico's banks.

1985 A major earthquake hits Mexico City.

1986 Mexico enters into GATT (General Agreement on Tariffs and Trade).

1987 Mexico begins the Economic Solidarity Pact, whose goal is to reduce inflation.

1988 Hurricane Gilbert strikes Mexico.

1989 The Brady Plan helps restructure Mexico's debt.

1991 Mexico signs a bilateral free-trade agreement with Chile to reduce tariffs.

1992 The North American Free Trade Agreement (NAFTA) is signed by Mexican President Salinas, U.S. President Bush, and Canadian Prime Minister Mulroney.

1994 NAFTA officially goes into effect.

1995 Inflation shoots to 52 percent in Mexico.

1997 Good economic measures help Mexico pay back $13.5 billion to the United States.

1998 Mexico exports $117.5 billion of manufactured goods.

1999 Mexican government passes the Mining Law Regulation to update mining procedures.

2000 Vicente Fox is elected president of Mexico; he promises to continue Mexico's economic growth.

2001 President Fox meets with U.S. President George W. Bush to discuss a cooperative relationship between the neighboring countries.

2002 Latin American leaders, including Mexico's Vicente Fox, meet in Argentina for the Global Alumni Conference to discuss technological and economic issues.

GLOSSARY

Assets Resources; money or items of value.

Bismuth A heavy, brittle, grayish white metal used in alloys and pharmaceutical drugs.

Celestite A white mineral.

Civil Having to do with citizens; a civil war is fought between citizens of the same country.

Conserve To avoid wasting or destruction.

Exile When a person is forced to leave his or her home.

Exports Goods or commodities shipped out of a country to other nations.

Fluorspar A transparent or translucent mineral used to make opaque glasses.

Graphite A soft black form of carbon that's used for the lead in pencils, in electrolytic anodes, and in nuclear reactors.

Imports Goods or commodities shipped into a country from other nations.

Inflation A rise in prices.

Interest rates The percentage at which borrowed or banked money earns an additional amount.

Kilowatt-hours A unit of energy equal to that used by 1000 watts in one hour.

Nationalism Pride in one's country.

Peso Mexican unit of money.

Petroleum Thick, almost black fluid that lies underneath the earth's surface; used to produce kerosene, gasoline, natural gas, and motor oil.

Promotion Advertising; encouraging the public to make use of a particular good or location.

Recession A period of diminished economic activity.

Sector A subdivision of society.

Tariffs A tax imposed by the government on imported or exported goods.

Unemployment rate The percentage of people in the population who are out of work.

FURTHER READING

Aspe, Pedro. *Economic Transformation the Mexican Way*. Cambridge, Mass.: The MIT Press, 1993.

Davila, Carlos and Miller, Rory. *Business History in Latin America: The Experience of Seven Countries*. Liverpool, England: Liverpool University Press, 1999.

Heath, Jonathan. *Mexico and the Sexenio Curse*. Washington, D.C.: The CSIS Press, 1999.

Lustig, Nora. *Mexico: The Remaking of an Economy*. Washington, D.C.: The Brookings Institution, 1992.

MacDonald, Scott B. and Fauriol, Georges A. *Fast Forward*. New Brunswick, N.J.: Transaction Publishers, 1999.

Mexico: A Travel Survival Kit. Berkeley, Calif.: Lonely Planet Publications, 1992.

Purcell, Susan Kaufman and Rubio, Luis. *Mexico Under Zedillo*. Boulder, Colo.: Lynne Rienner Publishers, 1998.

Randall, Laura. *Changing Structure of Mexico*. Armonk, N.Y.: M. E. Sharpe, 1996.

Roett, Riordian. *Mexico's Private Sector*. Boulder, Colo.: Lynne Rienner Publishers, 1998.

Russell, Philip L. *Mexico Under Salinas*. Austin, Tex.: Mexico Resource Center, 1994.

INTERNET RESOURCES

Legal Issues of Mexico and Business in Latin America
http://www.mexicolaw.com

Faces Behind the Label
http://www.behindthelabel.org

Information About Mexico
http://www.mexconnect.com

INDEX

PICTURE CREDITS

2: Corbis Images
3: Danny Lehman/Corbis
10: Wesley Bocxe/Newsmakers
13: Bettmann/Corbis
14: Bettmann/Corbis
16: Bettmann/Corbis
18: Reuters/Archive
21: Bettmann/Corbis
22: Richard Ellis/Archive
25: Wesley Bocxe/Newsmakers
28: Bettmann/Corbis
31: Bohemian Nomad Picturemakers/Corbis
32: Charles and Josette Lenars/Corbis
35: Sergio Dorantes/Corbis
36: Danny Lehman/Corbis
39: Corbis Images
40: Dan Guravich/Corbis
41: Phil Schermeister/Corbis
42: Corbis images
45: Bettmann/Corbis
46: Larry Lee Photography/Corbis
49: Vince Streano/Corbis
50: Corbis Images
53: Reuters NewMedia Inc./Corbis
54: Corbis Images
56: Richard Cummins/Corbis

Cover (front) Jeffrey W. Meyers/Corbis
(inset) Danny Lehman/Corbis
(back) Bettmann/Corbis

CONTRIBUTORS

Roger E. Hernández is the most widely syndicated columnist writing on Hispanic issues in the United States. His weekly column, distributed by King Features, appears in some 40 newspapers across the country, including the *Washington Post*, *Los Angeles Daily News*, *Dallas Morning News*, *Arizona Republic*, *Rocky Mountain News* in Denver, *El Paso Times*, and *Hartford Courant*. He is also the author of *Cubans in America*, an illustrated history of the Cuban presence in what is now the United States, from the early colonists in 16th-century Florida to today's Castro-era exiles. The book was designed to accompany a PBS documentary of the same title.

Hernández's articles and essays have been published in the *New York Times*, *New Jersey Monthly*, *Reader's Digest*, and *Vista Magazine*; he is a frequent guest on television and radio political talk shows, and often travels the country to lecture on his topic of expertise. Currently, he is teaching journalism and English composition at the New Jersey Institute of Technology in Newark, where he holds the position of writer-in-residence. He is also a member of the adjunct faculty at Rutgers University.

Hernández left Cuba with his parents at the age of nine. After living in Spain for a year, the family settled in Union City, New Jersey, where Hernandez grew up. He attended Rutgers University, where he earned a BA in Journalism in 1977; after graduation, he worked in television news before moving to print journalism in 1983. He lives with his wife and two children in Upper Montclair, New Jersey.

Erica Stokes is a freelance writer. Her work for children and young adults has been published in magazines, Web sites, software, and books. She currently resides in the Tennessee Valley of north Alabama.